Mysterious Monsters

Searching for the Loch Ness Monster

Jennifer Rivkin

PowerKiDS press

New York

Published in 2015 by The Rosen Publishing Group, Inc.
29 East 21st Street, New York, NY 10010

Produced for Rosen by BlueApple*Works* Inc.
Art Director: Tibor Choleva
Designer: Joshua Avramson
Photo Research: Jane Reid
Editor for BlueApple*Works*: Melissa McClellan
US Editor: Joshua Shadowens

Illustrations: Cover, p. 9, 10 left, 14 bottom, 16 top, 22–23 bottom, 24, 25, 26, 26–27 bottom T. Choleva; p. 4–5, 7 right Victor Habbick/Shutterstock; p. 8 right, 15 left, 19 Carlyn Iverson; p. 24 top Computer Earth/Shutterstock

Photo Credits: p. 1, 12, 14, 16, 18, 21 Fortean Picture Library; p.4–5 background Andrey Kuzmin/Shutterstock; p. 6 top, 26 top Circumnavigation/Shutterstock; p. 6 left Creative Jen Designs/Shutterstock; p. 6 right Anneka/Shutterstock; p. 7 left elementals/Shutterstock; p. 7 bottom Pincasso/Shutterstock; p. 8 top Viachaslau Kraskouski/Shutterstock; p. 8 left OSORIOartist/Shutterstock; p. 9 right stevehullphotography/Shutterstock; p. 10 top Thomas Nord/Shutterstock; p. 11 Hulton Archive/iStock; p. 12 top Everett Collection/Shutterstock; p. 12–13 background Molodec/Shutterstock; p. 14 top Dmytro Strelbytskyy/Dreamstime; p. 14 right Narimbur/Dreamstime; p. 15 right plasid/Shutterstock; p. 17 ©Craig W MacGregor, courtesy of; p. 18 top Song Heming/Shutterstock; p. 18–19 bottom ptashka/Shutterstock; p. 20 top argus/Shutterstock; p. 20 middle Kirsanov Valeriy Vladimirovich/Shutterstock; p. 20 bottom Elzbieta Sekowska/Shutterstock; p 20–21 bottom Dudarev Mikhail/Shutterstock; p. 22 top Mariusz Potocki/Shutterstock; p. 23 Marco Regalia/Dreamstime; p. 27 right Dan Exton/Shutterstock; p. 28 top stanalex/Shutterstock; p. 28 top right ra2studio/Shutterstock; p. 28 Andrew Lundquist/Shutterstock; p. 29 top Andre Goncalves/Shutterstock; p. 29 middle John Braid/Dreamstime; p. 29 bottom ags1973/Shutterstock; eyewitness tale boxes Theeradech Sanin/Shutterstock; paper background Fedorov Oleksiy/Shutterstock

Library of Congress Cataloging-in-Publication-Data

Rivkin, Jennifer, author.
 Searching for the Loch Ness monster / by Jennifer Rivkin.
     pages cm. — (Mysterious monsters)
 Includes index.
 ISBN 978-1-4777-7101-3 (library binding) — ISBN 978-1-4777-7102-0 (pbk.) —
 ISBN 978-1-4777-7103-7 (6-pack)
 1. Loch Ness monster—Juvenile literature. I. Title.
 QL89.2.L6R58 2015
 001.944—dc23
                          2013049389

Manufactured in the United States of America

CPSIA Compliance Information: Batch #WS14PK8 For Further Information contact: Rosen Publishing, New York, New York at 1-800-237-9932

Table of Contents

What Is the Loch Ness Monster?

Strange things have been happening in the waters of Loch Ness, in Northern Scotland, for as far back as people can remember. Over the years, hundreds of eyewitnesses have spotted something lurking in the loch. Most report seeing a giant creature rising out of the water or speeding across the lake and then disappearing back into the deep. They call this creature the Loch Ness Monster.

We have been told that monsters don't exist, but is this true? Could monsters really roam—or swim—the Earth?

▲ *The Loch Ness Monster is the official name of the creature. Throughout the years people living around the loch came to love the idea of having a monster in their midst. They have affectionately named their monster Nessie.*

In 1971, Father Gregory Brusey, a monk at Fort Augustus Abbey in Inverness-shire, Scotland, was walking in the garden by the loch when he and another man saw a head and neck of some strange animal sticking six feet (1.8 m) out of the water. It moved through the water and then descended back into the loch.

Unanswered Questions

With today's new technology and methods, researchers can answer questions about the Earth in ways our ancestors could not have imagined. Even with all of these tools at their fingertips, scientists have yet to solve one of the greatest mysteries of all time—does the Loch Ness Monster really exist?

Read on and decide for yourself.

LOCH NESS IN SCOTLAND

Loch Ness is a large, deep, freshwater loch in the Scottish Highlands near the city of Inverness. Loch is the Irish and Scottish **Gaelic** word for a lake or sea inlet. The loch is almost 23 miles (37 km) long, over 1.5 miles (2.4 km) wide at its widest point, and around 750 feet (229 m) deep. Because it is so deep, it holds more water than the total **volume** of water held in all the lakes in England and Wales combined. The loch is easily big enough for a large creature to live in it. The number of sightings over the years **indicate** there may be something there.

◀ *Inverness, meaning "Mouth of the River Ness," is a city in the Scottish Highlands. It is the northernmost city in the United Kingdom.*

LOCH NESS AND THE MONSTER

Reports of a monster lurking in the waters of Loch Ness, date back as far as the sixth century. Scottish **mythology** includes many stories of creatures that lurk in or near water. The early stories of a monster in Loch Ness are tied in with this mythology. It was not until 1933 that the Loch Ness Monster in the form it is now known became popular.

▲ *Many tourists flock to Loch Ness and Urquhart Castle on the Loch each year in the hopes of seeing Nessie. There are boat cruises on the loch and there is a museum and gift shop in the nearby town of Drumnadrochit.*

THE MYSTERY BEGINS

The first recorded account of a monster sighting in the loch took place over 1,000 years ago in 565 C.E. An Irish monk, named Saint Columba, was traveling in the area near the loch when he came across a group of locals burying a body by the river Ness. This is the river connecting Loch Ness to Inverness. They told Columba that a monster had attacked their friend while he was swimming out into the lake to retrieve his boat. Curious, the monk asked one of his followers to go into the lake and swim toward the boat. When the beast rose from the water to attack the man, Saint Columba formed the sign of the cross in the air and the beast fled.

◀ As recorded in ancient manuscripts, the exact words that Saint Columba used to scare off the beast were: "Thou shalt go no further, nor touch the man; return with all speed."

KELPIES

Saint Columba wasn't the first person to hear the tale of a monster in the water. For years before he visited there— and long after he left—the children of Scotland were told folktales about kelpies in the loch. Legend has it that kelpies were water spirits. They would come out of the lake disguised as beautiful horses, and enticed humans to ride them. Once a person mounted the horse, the kelpie's skin or saddle would hold the person tight, and the kelpie would take its victim into the water to drown.

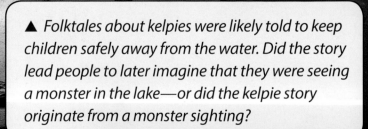

▲ Folktales about kelpies were likely told to keep children safely away from the water. Did the story lead people to later imagine that they were seeing a monster in the lake—or did the kelpie story originate from a monster sighting?

THE FIRST MODERN SIGHTINGS

Before the 1930s, Loch Ness was isolated because it lacked road access making it difficult to get to. When a road was eventually built along the lake, workers and tourists followed. . . and the sightings increased.

The year 1933 was a big year for Nessie. She became known around the world after John Mackay and his wife, Aldie, reported seeing a whale-like hump in the water when they were driving along a road on the north shore. They said that the beast had made a big disturbance in the water.

▶ On this page you can see an artistic reconstruction of what Mackay witnessed. There is not much chance that they saw a stranded whale in the loch. It would be almost impossible for a whale to enter the loch. If it wasn't a whale, what was it—Nessie?

OFFICIAL NAME

Soon, monster sightings in the lake began to attract the attention of newspapers in Scotland and across the globe. The creature finally got a name. According to the *Oxford English Dictionary*, 1933 saw the **coining** of the term Loch Ness Monster.

EYEWITNESS TALE

The Mackays weren't the only couple to see something strange near the loch in 1933. Published in the newspaper that year was the story of George Spicer and his wife. They told reporters they had seen a giant snail-like creature with a long narrow neck that was 4 feet (1.22 m) high and 25 feet (7.62 m) long. They did not see their monster in the loch. It crossed the road in front of their car before heading into the water on the other side.

▲ Nessie became a well-known celebrity in the 1930s. Reporters everywhere were busy collecting stories from eyewitnesses to publish in newspapers and magazines around the world.

NESSIE AND THE PAPARAZZI

Although she has become a celebrity, Nessie has proven to be camera shy over the years. People have spent hundreds of hours trying to capture her image, but few have managed to do so.

The first person to claim to have a picture of Nessie was Hugh Gray. In 1933, he produced a blurry image of a large, long-tailed animal on top of the water. The picture was published in many newspapers, but because it wasn't clear, it only added to the questions people had about whether or not there actually was a monster in Loch Ness.

▶ Hugh Gray was walking along the loch when he noticed unusual movements in the water. A large creature rose up from the lake. Gray took hurried pictures of it. What he captured showed what looked like a creature with a long tail and thick body on the surface of the water. The image is not clear, perhaps because the animal was splashing in the water.

THE SURGEON'S PHOTOGRAPH

The most famous photo of Nessie was submitted to the newspapers in 1934 by Dr. Robert Kenneth Wilson. The picture, which has been called *The Surgeon's Photograph* because the doctor did not want his name associated with it, looks like a shot of Nessie's neck and head sticking out of the water. This photo convinced many people that the monster was real.

▲ The Surgeon's Photograph *was the first published photograph that showed Nessie's head and neck sticking out of the loch's surface.*

NESSIE THE MOVIE STAR

In 1960, Tim Dinsdale made a film that was considered the most important piece of evidence for the existence of the Loch Ness Monster. Dinsdale carried out a one-person expedition in which he spent five days at the loch, searching for Nessie. On the last day, he spotted something and filmed it with his 16 mm camera. What he captured was a hump going through the water, leaving a **wake** behind it. Many people believe in the Loch Ness Monster because of what they saw on his film.

▲ Tim Dinsdale used a camera similar to the one above. While filming the moving object he noticed that the camera was about to run out of film. He decided to stop and save the last few feet of film. He wanted to get a clearer picture. He ran down the hill to get closer to the loch, hoping the creature would still be there swimming in the water. But when he reached the shore of the loch all he could see was the still surface of the water. The creature was gone.

Nessie or a Boat?

There has been a lot of debate about what Dinsdale actually captured in his film. Was it a boat? Was it an animal? To this day, no one can be sure. . . even the experts. British Intelligence, NASA engineers, and computer specialists have all tried to figure it out. In 1993, documentary filmmakers had Dinsdale's film digitally enhanced to try to prove that the image was a boat. The investigation only led to more questions and offered no proof either way.

Eyewitness Tale

In 1963, Hugh Ayton and three of his friends claimed to have seen three large humps and a neck sticking out of the water in the loch. The eyewitnesses followed the "monster" for about 1 mile (1.6 km) in Ayton's boat. They reported that the beast had a 6-foot (1.8 m)-long neck, a 40-foot (12.2 m)-long body, and humps that rose 4 feet (1.2 m) out of the water. Most interestingly, they say that the creature had a horse-like head and stared at them through a large, oval eye.

◀ *This reconstruction from a frame of Dinsdale's movie (left) shows something moving across the lake creating a wake behind it. Some skeptics say that it could have been a small boat which creates a similar wake when seen from a distance.*

Scientific Research

Dinsdale went monster hunting alone, but other scientists have tried working together to prove or disprove the existence of Nessie. There have been many projects and official research stations set up to find evidence.

The Loch Ness Investigation Bureau

In 1962, after the Dinsdale film was published, The Loch Ness Investigation Bureau was formed. The group ran months-long expeditions using several strategies to try to find Nessie. Much of the work was tedious and involved volunteers watching the surface of the water for hours on end with cameras ready. The group also used searchlights and manned submarines that had sonar.

▶ *The Loch Ness Investigation Bureau volunteers on high alert watching the surface in hopes of spotting Nessie. The Bureau never found the solid evidence they were looking for before they shut down in 1972.*

THE LOCH NESS PROJECT

Another group, The Loch Ness Project, was founded in 1978 and still exists today. Founder Adrian Shine encourages university students to study the lake and the monster controversy scientifically. They observe, sample, and record data on things like the water chemistry, sediment, and fish habitats in the loch. They have published many scientific research papers.

▲ The Loch Ness Centre & Exhibition opened over 30 years ago. Visitors can learn about 500 million years of history of Loch Ness and everything that there is to know about the famous Nessie legend.

UNDERWATER PICTURES

In the 1970s, photographers tried to capture pictures of the Loch Ness Monster with underwater cameras. It wasn't easy. Because of the chemistry of the soil surrounding the lake, the water is extremely murky and dark.

With technology that could detect underwater activity, Dr. Robert Rines and his team used a **submersible** camera with an attached floodlight to take pictures. The team captured some images—and many people's attention—with several of them. One picture showed what appeared to be the head and neck of a dinosaur-like creature.

▶ Dr. Robert Rines and his team launched numerous expeditions over several years trying to capture underwater pictures of the Loch Ness Monster.

GIANT FLIPPER

The most well-known pictures were of what appeared to be a flipper in different positions (as if it was moving). The picture was blurry because of the murkiness of the water, but it seemed to show a hindquarter, flipper, and part of the tail of a large animal with rough-textured skin of a greenish brown color. Experts estimated the flipper to be from six to eight feet (1.8–2.4 m) in length.

▲ *The flipper was shaped like a rhombus, or a diamond, which led naturalist Sir Peter Scott (who was on the expedition) to give Nessie the scientific name,* Nessiteras rhombopteryx.

SEARCHING WITH SONAR

Sonar is a method of using sound to detect objects under water, either by listening for the sound made by objects (like submarines) or by emitting pulses of sound and listening for their echo. The longer it takes for the echo to bounce back, the farther away the object is located. The sonar screen shows a rough picture of the object's size, shape, and speed.

▲ *Sonar equipment in various shapes and forms has long played an important role in seabed surveys, underwater investigations, and commercial fishing. But the real masters of using sonar waves are bats. They can catch small insects in complete darkness by listening to echoes bouncing back from their prey.*

Operation Deepscan

Because the water of Loch Ness is so murky, sonar has been an important tool for scientists searching for the monster. A few began using it in the loch in the 1950s, with limited results. One of the most elaborate sonar searches took place in 1987. It was called Operation Deepscan. The maneuver had 24 boats, spread across the width of the loch, using their sonar systems at the same time. Deepscan determined that there were large objects in the loch, but it was never clear exactly what they were. A similar experiment in 2003 was inconclusive.

Eyewitness Tale

In 2009, Jason Cooke claimed he saw the Loch Ness Monster on his computer in a satellite picture of the loch on Google Earth. The satellite picture of the loch showed a 65-foot (19.8 m) shape, which looked like a giant squid.

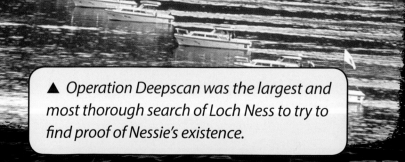

▲ Operation Deepscan was the largest and most thorough search of Loch Ness to try to find proof of Nessie's existence.

WHAT ELSE COULD IT BE?

Thousands of eyewitnesses claim to have seen the Loch Ness Monster. Sonar scans have shown large objects in the loch. Photos have captured strange shapes in the water. If it is not Nessie, what could they have seen?

Sonar may have picked up large schools of fish, rather than a lake monster. Perhaps eyewitnesses are seeing other animals and mistaking them for Nessie. Birds, seals, otters, or eels are all possibilities. Seals would explain the Nessie sightings on land. And the three-humped monster? That could be three large otters swimming together in a line.

▲ *Some people believe that Nessie is nothing but a big fish. The sturgeon is a big, sea-going fish that enters freshwater to breed and spawn. The sturgeon has a reptile-like appearance and can grow into a "monster" size. Lengths of 7–12 feet (2–3.5 m) are common. Some species can even grow up to 18 feet (5.5 m). The sturgeon's long snout could give the appearance of the characteristic Nessie neck.*

Confusing Shapes

It may be that witnesses are seeing not a monster but a floating tree trunk (or one rising from the bottom of the loch), a pod of algae, boat wakes, underwater waves, or gas being released from the **fault** under the loch. Maybe it's as simple as shadows playing tricks or reflections of the mountains or rocks.

Did You Know?

There could be a LOG-Ness Monster? Scientist Dr. Maurice Burton believes that the sightings of Nessie may be caused by a natural phenomenon involving rotting trees. Dead pine trees along the shore of the loch fall into the water and sink down to the bottom where they rot. This leads to a build up of gases in the log. At first, the gas is trapped inside the log by a glue-like substance called resin. When the gas pressure builds up enough, it can pop off the resin cap at one end of the log, which can propel the wood through the water, enough to break through the surface. Could this be what eyewitnesses have seen?

▲ *Large schools of fish can look like one huge creature when picked up on sonar screens. Viewed from a distance, floating tree trunks in the mist can look like slow-moving water monsters.*

THE PLESIOSAUR THEORY

Some of those who believe in the existence of the Loch Ness Monster think that it is an ancestor of the *Plesiosaurus,* a prehistoric aquatic reptile with a small head and long neck, which is thought to have become extinct 65 million years ago with the dinosaurs. Fossil records of the plesiosaur show that it looked similar to the descriptions of Nessie.

▶ Plesiosaurus *was a large water reptile that lived during the early part of the Jurassic Period. Its small head, long and slender neck, and broad turtle-like body made it look like a present-day Nessie. However, the* Plesiosaurus *was rather small for a monster. It grew only to a length of about 11 feet (3.5 m).*

Could It Be Possible?

Many scientists argue that the plesiosaur theory is impossible. Firstly, there would not be enough food in the lake to sustain a plesiosaur. Secondly, plesiosaurs lived in warm water because they were cold-blooded reptiles and could never have survived in the loch. Most importantly, 10,000 years ago during the last **ice age**, Loch Ness was a frozen block of ice!

Did You Know?

Loch Ness is a **tectonic lake**, which means that it was formed by the movement of the Earth's crust. About 400 million years ago, earthquakes caused the ground around Loch Ness to split and later shift apart. Then during the last ice age (10,000 years ago), glaciers chiseled a steep trench in the area, which would later become Loch Ness.

▲ Although it is unlikely that plesiosaurs are the cause of monster sightings, it is not entirely impossible. Other creatures that were thought to be extinct for millions of years have been discovered living in modern times. The coelacanth, a fish that was believed to be extinct 65 million years ago, was found in 1938 in the waters near South Africa.

NESSIE'S COUSINS?

Nessie is hardly alone in her ability to attract attention as there are dozens of other lakes in which monsters have been sighted. Lake monster sightings have been reported across the globe. North America has its fair share of lake monsters.

For example—Old Greeny, a 35-foot (10.7 m) sea serpent, is said to live in Cayuga Lake, New York. There have been reports of Greeny from 1887–1979.

A more unique-looking monster is the eel-pig of Herrington Lake, Kentucky. It is described as 15-feet (4.6 m) long and shaped like an eel, but with a curly tail and the face of a pig. That would be an interesting sight!

◀ *The monster of Herrington Lake has been described as a pig out of a horror movie. Witnesses claimed that it was 15 feet (4.6 m) long and moving as fast as a motor boat.*

Ogopogo Monster

Since the nineteenth century, people have reported seeing a lake monster in Lake Okanagan in south-central British Columbia, Canada. The serpent-like creature has a head like a horse and humps on its body. Unlike the Loch Ness Monster, sightings of this **cryptid** have been reported almost every year, and a prominent insurance company even offered a large sum of money for proof of Ogopogo. However, no proof has been provided, because the only evidence is limited to blurry photographs, and the tall tales of the sea creature that inhabits the 80-mile (135 km)-long lake.

Lake monster sightings have been reported in other countries too. Sweden and Argentina also have their own lake monsters. Are they all Nessie's cousins or just another myth?

▼ *Ogopogo has been allegedly seen by First Nations people since the 19th century. The most common description of Ogopogo is a 40- to 50-foot-long (12 to 15 m) sea serpent.*

WHAT DO YOU THINK?

Is it possible that all of the people who claim to have seen Nessie have imagined it or seen an **optical illusion**? Maybe. There has never been a carcass or skeleton the shape and size of the Loch Ness Monster found in or around the loch. Most scientists believe that the monster is a myth.

Contrary to those beliefs are hundreds of people from all walks of life who are certain they have seen the Loch Ness Monster. Reports have come from monks, doctors, scientists, police officers, farmers, and more. Nessie has been sighted from fishing boats and from land. Whether a myth or a real creature, the stories keep coming.

▶ *Loch Ness' waters are vast, and its secrets deep. Some people believe in the monster lurking there, some people do not. But as long as there is a chance to see Nessie in the lake people will keep looking.*

HOAXES OR NOT

Although there have been some hoaxes related to the creature and there are some alternative explanations, does that mean that there can't be an unidentified animal living in the waters of Loch Ness? After all, the lake is deep and dark making it the perfect hiding place for a monster.

Could it be possible that the Loch Ness Monster really does exist? You be the judge. Maybe one day you can visit Loch Ness to investigate it for yourself.

▲ *There are many interesting sights and attractions to entertain visitors coming to Loch Ness. One of the most popular ones are boat cruises across the loch. Everybody hopes to see Nessie and, better yet, get pictures of her!*

GLOSSARY

accomplices (uh-KAHM-plus-ez) People who work with or help someone who is doing something wrong or illegal.

coining (KOIN-ing) To create a new word or phrase that other people begin to use.

cryptid (KRIHP-tid) A creature or plant whose existence has been suggested but is not recognized by scientific consensus.

fault (FAWLT) A crack in the Earth's crust.

Gaelic (GAY-lik) The Celtic language of Scotland and Ireland.

hoax (HOHKS) To trick into believing or accepting as genuine something false and often preposterous.

ice age (YS AYJ) Any geologic period during which thick ice sheets covered vast areas of land.

inconclusive (in-kon-KLOO-siv) Leading to no conclusion or definite result.

indicate (IN-duh-kayt) To show that something may be true.

mythology (mih-THAH-luh-jee) A collection of myths, which are beliefs believed by many but which have no proof of being true.

optical illusion (OP-tih-kul ih-LOO-zhun) Something that looks different from what it is: something that you seem to see but that is not really there.

submersible (sub-MUR-sih-bul) Capable of being put under water.

tectonic lake (tek-TAH-nik LAYK) A lake formed by the movement of the large sections of the Earth's crust. These lakes typically form at fault lines where plates meet and earthquakes are more common.

volume (VOL-yoom) An amount of space that is filled with something.

wake (WAYK) The track left by a moving body (as a ship) in a fluid (as water).

FOR MORE INFORMATION

FURTHER READING

Beaumont, Steve. *Drawing Plesiosaurus and Other Ocean Dinosaurs*.
    Drawing Dinosaurs. New York: PowerKids Press, 2010.

Regan, Lisa. *Urban Myths and Legendary Creatures*. Monsters and Myths.
    New York: Gareth Stevens, 2011.

Robert, Steven. *The Loch Ness Monster!* Jr. Graphic Monster Stories.
    New York: PowerKids Press, 2012.

WEBSITES

Due to the changing nature of Internet links, PowerKids Press has developed an online list of websites related to the subject of this book. This site is updated regularly. Please use this link to access the list:

www.powerkidslinks.com/mymo/loch/

INDEX